Ramadan

ABDO
Publishing Company

A Buddy Book
by
Julie Murray

VISIT US AT
www.abdopublishing.com

Published by ABDO Publishing Company, 8000 West 78th Street, Edina, Minnesota 55439.

Copyright © 2012 by Abdo Consulting Group, Inc. International copyrights reserved in all countries. No part of this book may be reproduced in any form without written permission from the publisher. Buddy Books™ is a trademark and logo of ABDO Publishing Company.

Printed in the United States of America, North Mankato, Minnesota.
052011
092011

♲ PRINTED ON RECYCLED PAPER

Coordinating Series Editor: Rochelle Baltzer
Editor: Sarah Tieck
Contributing Editors: Megan M. Gunderson, BreAnn Rumsch, Marcia Zappa
Graphic Design: Denise Esner
Cover Photograph: *Shutterstock*: Paul Cowan.
Interior Photographs/Illustrations: *Alamy*: Louise Batalla Duran (p. 11); *AP Photo*: Mohammed Ballas (p. 22), Mohammad Saijad (p. 17); *Getty Images*: KHALED DESOUKI/AFP (p. 19), ROMEO GALAD/AFP (p. 15); *Glow Images*: Robert Harding (p. 5), Kay Maeritz/LOOK-foto (p. 13); *iStockphoto*: ©iStockphoto.com/afby71afby71 (p. 9); *PhotoEdit*: Michael Newman (p. 21); *Photo Researchers, Inc.*: Larry Landolfi (p. 7); *Shutterstock*: afaizal (p. 9).

Library of Congress Cataloging-in-Publication Data

Murray, Julie, 1969-
  Ramadan / Julie Murray.
    p. cm. -- (Holidays)
  ISBN 978-1-61783-041-9
  1. Ramadan--Juvenile literature. I. Title.
  BP186.4.R448 2012
  297.3'62--dc22
                              2011002287

Table of Contents

What Is Ramadan? 4

New Moon 6

A Special Book 8

Honoring Allah 12

Day by Day 14

Prayer 16

Ramadan Today 20

Id al-Fitr 22

Important Words 23

Web Sites 23

Index 24

What Is Ramadan?

Ramadan is a sacred month in the **Muslim** calendar. During this month, Muslims **fast**, pray, and read the **Koran**.

Ramadan is the ninth month of the **Islamic** year. The Muslim calendar is based on the changing moon. So, Ramadan can take place during different seasons.

Islam started in what is now Saudi Arabia. But today, people all over the world follow Islam.

SYRIA
JORDAN
ISRAEL
IRAQ
IRAN
EGYPT
SAUDI ARABIA
■ Medina
■ Mecca
Red Sea
KUWAIT
QATAR
UNITED ARAB EMIRATES
OMAN
SUDAN
ERITREA
YEMEN
DJIBOUTI
SOMALIA
Arabian Sea
ETHIOPIA

N
W E
S

Prayer is an important part of Islam.

New Moon

Ramadan begins with the ninth new moon of the **Islamic** year. The moon has a cycle. Over about 30 days, its shape appears to change. Sometimes the entire moon can be seen. Other times, none or only part of it can be seen.

During Ramadan, the moon completes one full cycle. Ramadan starts and ends when the first sliver of a crescent moon can be seen (*top left*).

A Special Book

Muslims have observed Ramadan since the time of Muhammad. Muhammad was a **prophet** who lived between AD 570 and 632.

In 610, Muhammad began getting messages from **Allah** through an angel. He shared Allah's messages with others. In this way, Muhammad formed **Islam**. Over time, Allah's messages were written in the **Koran**.

Muhammad was born in Mecca (*bottom*) and died in Medina (*top*). These cities are still important places for Muslims. They are in what is now Saudi Arabia.

The Kaaba (*center*) is a sacred building in Mecca.

Muhammad received the first parts of the **Koran** during Ramadan. So, **Muslims** remember and honor this special month.

Many Muslims read the entire Koran during Ramadan. The Koran has 30 parts, which teach Muslims how **Allah** wants them to live.

At first the Koran was only in the Arabic language. Today, there are copies in many languages.

Honoring Allah

Fasting is an important part of Ramadan. **Muslims** fast to honor the gifts **Allah** has given them. They also fast to understand other people's suffering.

During Ramadan, most Muslims fast in the daylight hours. Very young children do not fast. People who are old, sick, pregnant, or traveling also do not fast.

In Muslim countries, many markets and restaurants close during the day for Ramadan. Instead, food is sold at night.

Day by Day

During Ramadan, **Muslims** begin each day with suhoor (suh-HOOR). Suhoor is a special meal eaten before sunrise. Muslims do not eat or drink again until after sunset.

Each night after sunset, Muslims gather together to break their fast. They eat a meal called iftar (ihf-tahr). It can be served at home or at a **mosque**.

Each family makes the iftar meal according to their preferences.

Iftar often begins with dates and water. This is what Muhammad ate long ago. A larger meal follows.

Prayer

Prayer is an important part of **Islam**. Islam requires **Muslims** to pray five times each day. There are prayers at dawn, midday, afternoon, sunset, and evening.

When they pray, Muslims face Mecca. They stand and bow to the ground. They often use rugs so their area for prayer is clean.

Muslims often pray in groups at mosques.

During Ramadan, many **Muslims** say special prayers each night. These prayers are called tarawih (tah-RAH-wee). For tarawih, Muslims speak a chapter of the **Koran**, often from memory.

The Night of Power is toward the end of Ramadan. On this night, many Muslims pray all night. They do this in honor of Muhammad receiving the Koran.

Muslims around the world gather in mosques for tarawih.

Ramadan Today

Today, some families observe Ramadan at home. Others attend **mosques** for prayers, such as tarawih.

Ramadan remains a very important month for **Muslims**. It is a time to think about **Allah** and to be grateful for one's blessings.

When Ramadan ends, Muslims are excited. The next three days are filled with food and fun. These days are called Id al-Fitr.

Id al-Fitr

Id al-Fitr is a time to have fun. Families visit friends. They give gifts to children and money to the poor.

Muslims also enjoy feasts. Many eat foods such as cake. Other foods depend on what a family likes and where they live.

People honor Id al-Fitr in different ways around the world. In some places, there are carnival rides!

Important Words

Allah the name for God in the religion of Islam.

fast to go without eating food.

Islam a religion based on a belief in Allah as God and Muhammad as his prophet.

Koran (kuh-RAHN) also spelled Quran or Qur'an. The Koran is the word of Allah and the sacred book of Islam, which is the religion of Muslims.

mosque (MAHSK) a building where Muslims worship.

Muslim a person who practices Islam.

prophet (PRAH-fuht) someone who brings messages to others from a god.

Web Sites

To learn more about Ramadan,
visit ABDO Publishing Company online. Web sites about Ramadan are featured on our Book Links page. These links are routinely monitored and updated to provide the most current information available.

www.abdopublishing.com

Index

Allah **8, 10, 12, 20**

Arabic.............................. **11**

fasting **4, 12, 14**

food **13, 14, 15, 21, 22**

Id al-Fitr **21, 22**

iftar **14, 15**

Kaaba **9**

Koran **4, 8, 10, 11, 18**

Mecca **9, 16**

Medina..........................**9**

moon..................... **4, 6, 7**

mosque........**14, 17, 19, 20**

Muhammad......... **8, 9, 10, 15, 18**

Muslim calendar **4, 6**

Night of Power.............. **18**

prayer................. **4, 5, 16, 17, 18, 20**

Saudi Arabia.............. **5, 9**

suhoor......................... **14**

tarawih.............**18, 19, 20**